T0146840

THE PRACTICAL STRATEGIES SERIES
IN AUTISM EDUCATION

---

series editors
FRANCES A. KARNES & KRISTEN R. STEPHENS

Gifted Children With Autism Spectrum Disorders

Maureen Neihart, Psy.D.,
& Kenneth Poon, Ph.D.

Routledge
Taylor & Francis Group

NEW YORK AND LONDON

First published 2009 by Prufrock Press Inc.

Published 2021 by Routledge
605 Third Avenue, New York, NY 10017
2 Park Square, Milton Park, Abingdon, Oxon OX14 4RN

Routledge is an imprint of the Taylor & Francis Group, an informa business

Copyright © 2009 by Frances A. Karnes
and Kristen R. Stephens-Kozak

All rights reserved. No part of this book may be reprinted or reproduced or utilised in any form or by any electronic, mechanical, or other means, now known or hereafter invented, including photocopying and recording, or in any information storage or retrieval system, without permission in writing from the publishers.

Notice:
Product or corporate names may be trademarks or registered trademarks, and are used only for identification and explanation without intent to infringe.

ISBN 13: 978-1-59363-373-8 (pbk)

Contents

Series Preface

The Practical Strategies Series in Autism Education offers teachers, counselors, administrators, parents, and other interested parties up-to-date information on a variety of issues pertaining to the characteristics, diagnosis, treatment, and education of students with autism spectrum disorders. Each guide addresses a focused topic and is written by an individual with authority on the issue. Several guides have been published. Among the titles are:

- *An Introduction to Children With Autism*
- *Diagnosis and Treatment of Children With Autism Spectrum Disorders*
- *Educational Strategies for Children With Autism Spectrum Disorders*

For a current listing of available guides within the series, please contact Prufrock Press at 800-998-2208 or visit http://www.prufrock.com.

My son received a very late diagnosis of Asperger syndrome (AS). He was 13 years old. He had been called many different things throughout his life. Words such as "eccentric," "gifted," and "shy" come to mind. I was always on the sidelines, though, hoping that they were right and I was wrong. It had always seemed to me to be something more, almost inexplicable or intangible. I would question certain inconsistencies, clumsiness, extreme discomfort around strangers, near hysteria at changes in routine, and most important, a complete lack of friendships. On the other hand, mastery scores would be quoted to me. Report cards were waved joyfully. There was a sense of what could be the problem with a mind like this. The answer to that is plenty. (Rietschel, 2000, p. 448)

Autism spectrum disorders (ASD) are developmental disorders characterized by severe deficits in social communication and restricted patterns of interests and behaviors. Prevalence estimates have increased considerably in the last decade, and

ASD is now considered to be the fastest growing disability in the United States, affecting approximately 1 in every 150 children ages 3–10 (Centers for Disease Control and Prevention, 2007). Boys are 3–4 times as likely as girls to be diagnosed. Separate prevalence rates for gifted children with ASD are not available, although Foley Nicpon, Assouline, and O'Brien's (2007) study suggested that the rates are similar among gifted boys and girls.

Like other twice-exceptional children, gifted children with autism spectrum disorders are sometimes forced to choose between addressing the concerns of one exceptionality over another, but this is occurring less and less as dedicated teachers and informed parents collaborate to create environments and programming that supports the child's individual profile of abilities. The aim of this volume is to describe instructional and behavior management strategies for the most common challenges teachers face with gifted children with ASD so that the abilities of these children can be developed to their fullest potential.

Gifted children with ASD are similar to other children with ASD in that they lack the ability to infer information about the internal states of others. They also are often described as having restricted interests, pedantic and monotonic speech, poor social communication (including poor eye contact), little emotional understanding, and poor motor planning. Gifted students with ASD typically have fine motor difficulties, resulting in poor handwriting and difficulty with certain tools in science and technology. Their speech is odd, often pedantic, characterized by one-sided conversations that focus on narrowly defined topics that are of intense interest to them. They have great difficulty with the give and take of normal conversation, and often violate speech boundaries by interrupting, failing to respond, or lecturing excessively. They have trouble stopping themselves once they start talking. They may be highly verbal and possess exceptional vocabularies, but they are unable to make their speech work for them. They convey information, but not in a way that makes connections. They talk at people rather than with them. They understand and use language literally rather than figuratively, missing many of the nuances of social interactions. Their information may be highly accurate, but they fail to understand the tone with which something is said. They exhibit a rigid inflexibility in thought and behavior that is puzzling and problematic at both home and school. However, all of these traits vary widely among children with ASD in their severity and intensity.

In comparison to other gifted children, gifted children with ASD have significant executive function deficits and these cause them ongoing difficulties with multitasking, organization, and auditory processing. Multitasking requires rapid information processing, but children with ASD are typically slow information processors. This means that it takes them longer than other children, and much longer than other gifted children, to do two things at the same time. For instance, listening to the teacher and following her instructions while taking notes is likely to be extremely difficult. An assignment that involves reading and analyzing an essay and writing a short response may take these students 2–3 times longer than their classmates. It may be nearly impossible for some students to participate in a lively group discussion because they can't track or process the comments of so many people at once.

However, like other gifted children, gifted children with ASD *want* to work quickly. If they are in accelerated classes or in classes with many other gifted children, they may feel pressured to keep up and be able to complete similar quantities of work in the same amount of time. They may become very frustrated when they are unable to do so, and peers or adults who do not understand the extreme discrepancies and curious nature of their abilities also may inadvertently press them to work more quickly than they can. Behavioral, emotional, and academic problems are likely to ensue when peers and teachers fail to appreciate their slower processing speed and push gifted students with ASD to multitask or to accomplish more than they can in the time provided. Teachers are most helpful when they normalize the students' slower processing speed, anticipate the difficulties they will face with a lesson or activity, and adjust expectations.

Although there are no data yet to support the idea that gifted children with ASD are bullied, teased, or marginalized more than other kinds of exceptional children, it is easy to appreciate how vulnerable they may be to such behavior. The idiosyncratic nature of their interests and abilities and the gross difficulties they face following even the most basic social conventions make them an easy target for bullies.

Research on gifted children with ASD in particular is extremely limited, but a recent study sponsored by the Belin–Blank Center at the University of Iowa helps us to understand the ways in which these children may be different from other gifted children without ASD and from other gifted children with other kinds of disabilities (Assouline, Foley Nicpon, Colangelo, & O'Brien, 2007; Foley Nicpon et al., 2007). Results of their comprehensive assessments with 36 children with ASD revealed enormous discrepancies in the profiles of abilities. The greatest discrepancy was the difference between their cognitive abilities and social competence. Overall reasoning ability fell in the superior range (97th percentile and above) while overall socialization fell in the 5th percentile. Not a *single child* in the Belin–Blank study scored in the average range for social functioning. It is the enormity of these discrepancies that distinguishes gifted children with ASD from other children with ASD and makes them especially challenging to teach. These discrepancies are very confusing to those who don't understand ASD.

In addition to the cognitive–social skills discrepancy, more than three fourths of the parents in the Belin–Blank study said that their children had difficulties with global adaptive skills. Also, parents and teachers reported similar views of the child's abilities but these views differed markedly from the children's self-reports. Specifically, the children viewed themselves as more capable than did parents and teachers. For instance, 83% of the children reported average self-esteem scores and 82% did not report relationship concerns. The odd profile of their abilities, and the huge discrepancies among them, has the greatest implications for instruction, educational placement, and postsecondary planning. The questions most commonly faced by schools and families are:

1. What is the best educational placement for this child?
2. How can the child's strengths be nurtured while accommodating the disabilities and coping with the child's idiosyncratic behaviors?
3. How will planning and preparing for this child's postsecondary training be addressed?

As a result of their advanced cognitive abilities, gifted children often demonstrate an awareness of self and others that is more advanced than that of their same-age peers (Gross, 1993; Janos & Robinson, 1985; Silverman, 1993). Even at relatively young ages, gifted children are aware that they are different from other children their age, and they seek friendships with older children who mirror their abilities and interests (Gross, 2002; Silverman, 1993). In contrast, gifted children with ASD are remarkably unaware of how others view them and typically initiate few social contacts with peers, even when they desire friendships.

Any efforts to plan effective intervention must begin with a comprehensive assessment. Only psychologists, psychiatrists, and physicians can make a diagnosis of ASD, but many professionals are involved with the initial assessment that guides educational planning and instruction. ASD can be reliably identified in children by about age 3, and studies suggest that even infants with ASD can be accurately identified (National Institute of Mental Health [NIMH], 2008). Assessment includes a developmental and family history, a semistructured interview with the child and/or his or her parents, and testing that clarifies the child's cognitive abilities and personality style. The purpose of the assessment is to delineate the individual child's unique profile of strengths and weaknesses and to generate a plan that recommends interventions and supports that will facilitate the child's optimal social functioning and achievement.

It is important that the assessment be conducted by a multidisciplinary team because ASD is a complex disorder with wide variability and a high incidence of co-occurrence with other conditions. Assessment is needed not only to profile the child's unique pattern of strengths and weaknesses, but also to identify and rule out other frequently co-occurring conditions. During assessment, measures are used that provide a detailed breakdown of the child's various strengths and weaknesses rather than just a composite score. Table 1 presents the domains that should be addressed, with recommended instruments for assessing each.

Table 1

Domains and Recommended Instruments

Domain	Recommended Instruments	Author and Publisher
Intellectual Ability	Wechsler Intelligence Scale for Children (WISC-IV)	Wechsler (2003); available from Pearson Assessment at http://www.pearsonassess.com
	Cognitive Abilities Test (CogAT)	D. F. Lohman and E. P. Hagen (2001); available from Riverside Publishing at http://www.riverpub.com
Achievement	Woodcock-Johnson III Tests of Achievement	R. W. Woodcock, K. S. McGrew, and N. Mather (2001); available from Riverside Publishing at http://www.riverpub.com
Adaptive Behavior	Vineland Adaptive Behavior Scales–II	S. S. Sparrow, D. V. Cicchetti, and D. A. Balla (1984); available from Pearson Assessment at http://www.pearsonassessments.com
	Behavior Assessment System for Children, Second Edition (BASC-2)	C. R. Reynolds and R. W. Kamphaus (2004); available from Pearson Assessment at http://www.pearsonassessments.com
Communication	Test of Pragmatic Language, Second Edition (TOPL-2)	D. Phelps-Terasaki and T. Phelps-Gunn (2007); available from Pro-Ed at http://www.proedinc.com
	Clinical Evaluation of Language Fundamentals (CELF-4)	E. H. Wiig, W. A. Secord, and E. Semel (2004); available from Pearson Assessment at http://www.pearsonassess.com
Visual-Motor	Beery-Buktenica Developmental Test of Visual-Motor Integration, Fifth Edition (Beery VMI)	K. E. Beery, N. A. Buktenica, and N. Beery (2004); available from Pearson Assessments at http://www.pearsonassessments.com
	Grooved Peg Board Test	Available from U.S. Medical Supplies at http://www.usmedicalsupplies.com
Autism Symptoms	Autism Diagnostic Observation Schedule (ADOS)	C. Lord, M. Rutter, P. C. DiLavore, and S. Risi (1989); available from Western Psychological Services at http://www.wpspublish.com
	Autism Diagnostic Interview–Revised (ADI-R)	M. Rutter, A. LeCouteur, and C. Lord (2003); available from Western Psychological Services at http://www.wpspublish.com
	Childhood Autism Rating Scale (CARS)	E. Schopler, R. J. Reichler, and B. Ro (1980); available from Pearson Assessments at http://www.pearsonassessments.com

Educational Strategies and Interventions

Following a thorough assessment, the plan for teaching gifted children with autism spectrum disorders begins with general information and support. How do we know what helps these children? Instructional decisions rely primarily on empirical research regarding:

- twice-exceptional children in general,
- children with ASD in general, and
- gifted children with ASD in particular.

In addition, a growing consensus in the literature concerning "what works" with these children should guide decisions about interventions and supports.

Although interventions for individual concerns may vary a great deal from one child to the next, there are two guiding principles to keep in mind when developing individual education plans for gifted children with ASD. The first is to provide an appropriate level of academic challenge. All gifted children need to work at their edge of competence in their areas of strengths and interests. A child's behavioral or emotional characteristics should never be used as a reason to keep the child busy with work he or she already has mastered. However, this doesn't mean that all gifted children with ASD should be placed in their school's gifted program. A school's gifted program, or an accelerated class or program, is not always the best fit for a gifted child with ASD.

There are many ways to meet a child's need for challenge in the curriculum, including advanced classes, online courses, mentorships, and independent studies. What is essential is that the child's talent be developed through systematic instruction. Research has demonstrated that an appropriate level of challenge is necessary not only for talent development and high academic achievement, but also for healthy social and emotional functioning (Neihart, 2007). It may not always be possible for gifted children with ASD to participate in their school's gifted program, seminars, or summer camps, but there should always be provisions for challenge in his or her areas of strength.

The second general principle is to make developing social competence a high priority. Given that the research on twice-exceptional children suggests that social and emotional functioning is the key to long-term success (Reis, Neu, & McGuire, 1997), and that the research on resilience in children identifies supportive relationships as the single best predictor of long-term positive outcomes for children raised with adversity (Luthar, 1991; Werner & Smith, 1992), it is imperative to aggressively and systematically work to develop a gifted child with ASD's social competence. This is not something that can be overlooked. It should be a priority along with the provision of academic challenge.

School personnel sometimes are tempted to work around a child's social deficits (speech and behavior) and cope with them as best they can, but failing to develop his or her social competence will seriously compromise his or her long-term success, adult achievement, and potential for satisfying relationships and healthy adjustment (Gross, 2004; Neihart, Reis, Robinson & Moon, 2002; Reis et al., 1997).

Beyond these two broad guiding principles, much has been written in recent years concerning interventions for children with ASD, although many of the claims made in the literature have yet to be empirically validated (Neihart, 2000, 2001; Stewart, 2002). Following is a discussion of four areas of concern that are the origins of many of the problems that keep gifted children with ASD from realizing their full potential: (1) sensory integration, (2) coping with transitions and change, (3) social competence, and (4) organization.

Coping With Sensory Integration Problems

One little-understood difficulty that is experienced by students with ASD is the unusual manner by which they perceive incoming stimuli. This section explores the difficulties experienced by students with ASD and suggests ways these difficulties may be prevented or managed.

Nature of Sensory Integration Problems
Most people are familiar with the five senses, but may have less understanding of two additional senses: proprioceptive and vestibular (Cook & Dunn, 1998). The proprioceptive sense refers to the extent to which individuals have an understanding of their body in space. The vestibular sense refers to the sense of balance.

Research into the sensory processing of people with ASD (e.g., Rogers, Hepburn, & Wehner, 2003) suggests that most people with ASD perceive sensory information differently. In contrast to other gifted children who often experience sensory sensitivities (Capps & Gere, 1999; Silverman, 1993), gifted children with ASD often are faced with sensory processing difficulties that result in emotional or behavioral problems in the classroom if these difficulties are not understood and accommodated. Specifically, some may overperceive some sensations (i.e., hypersensitive) whereas others may underperceive sensations (i.e., hyposensitive). Table 2 illustrates how hyper- and hyposensitivity to sensory stimuli may look in a school environment. Keep in mind that some children with ASD may be both hyper- as well as hyposensitive to specific senses.

Strategies for Preventing Sensory Integration Problems

The first step in managing sensory integration difficulties is prevention. There are three broad strategies:

1. understand the student's sensory needs,
2. plan the student's placement and classroom layout, and
3. involve classmates.

Understand the student's sensory needs. It's impossible to prevent what one doesn't understand. It is important to know what the child's sensory difficulties are. For instance, having a whiteboard may meet the needs of a student hypersensitive to the tactile feel of chalkboards, but may trigger many episodes of challenging behaviors for a student who is hypersensitive to the smell of whiteboard markers.

Plan the student's placement and classroom layout. When possible, classrooms should be designed to remove or at least reduce the types of stimuli to which a student with ASD may be hypersensitive. In particular, the visual environment needs to be managed.

Colorful classroom decorations, product displays, and lighting (especially fluorescent lights) are potential distracters for some students with ASD. Similarly, auditory distraction should be minimized. Examples include ceiling fans that squeak, chairs or classroom desks that grate on the floor, old fluorescent light tubes that strobe and crackle, and air conditioners that emit low-frequency vibrations. The olfactory and tactile environments also need attention. For instance, smells from musty curtains, sounds of classroom aquariums, and the heating and cooling levels of classrooms need to be considered. However, it is typically not feasible or possible to ameliorate all forms of sensory stimulus. In such cases, it will be necessary to consider the classroom layout and student placement.

Seating students away from sources of stimuli they find offending or distracting (e.g., a computer if the sound of the cooling fan distracts the student) may help reduce their impact. In addition, some students with ASD (particularly those with hypersensitive tactile systems) benefit from decreased proximity

Table 2
How Students With Sensory Integration
Difficulties May Behave

Sensory System	Potential Behaviors Related to Hypersensitive Perception	Potential Behaviors Related to Hyposensitive Perception	Samples Strategies to Cope or to Develop Integration
Visual	Easily distracted by bulletin boards and classroom decoration	Flicking pen repetitively in front of eyes; looks at spinning objects	1. Let the child wear sunglasses in class 2. Use a three-walled cubicle to reduce distractions 3. Place student in front row 4. Eliminate clutter in the classroom 5. Let the child suggest alternatives to activities he or she finds overstimulating
Auditory	Showing extreme reactions (e.g., cupping ears) to various sounds; easily distracted by background noise (e.g., hum of fluorescent lights, fish tank bubbler)	Sticking a finger into the ear while making vocalizations; not responding to name; turns volume up loud when listening to the radio	1. Let the child wear sound protection (e.g., earplugs, earphones, etc.) 2. Place child away from any equipment that buzzes or hums 3. Excuse child from participation in loud activities like assemblies, indoor recess, and pep rallies 4. Cover hard surfaces in the classroom with carpet or cloth to absorb sound
Tactile	Refusal to wear specific fabrics; overreacting to light touch from others (e.g., accidental shoulder rubs); disliking dirty hands	Asking for hugs; chewing on objects	1. Let the child be last in line; come to school early or late to avoid crowds 2. Permit greater physical proximity from peers 3. Encourage child to rub variety of objects against his skin 4. Include sand play, water play, or finger painting in the classroom 5. Let child handle pets in the classroom 6. Provide back rubs, shoulder massage, etc., with trusted adult at regular intervals throughout the day

Sensory System	Potential Behaviors Related to Hypersensitive Perception	Potential Behaviors Related to Hyposensitive Perception	Samples Strategies to Cope or to Develop Integration
Olfactory	Atypical avoidance of situations with specific smells	Bringing objects (or people) in the environment to the nose and sniffing	
Gustatory	Atypical avoidance of food (even traces) with specific tastes; frequent gagging; not wanting to mix foods when eating	Lifting objects in the environment to the mouth and tasting them; overeating	
Proprioceptive	Poor coordination; clumsiness; poor posture	Frequent "accidental" knocking into furniture and others	1. Make weighted vest for child to wear 2. Use joint squeeze at regular intervals during the day to de-stress: using slow, firm pressure, push and pull muscles near major joints. 3. Let child carry loads of books, supplies, etc., to and from classes 4. Provide opportunities to manipulate small objects: puzzles, LEGOs, science equipment, etc.
Vestibular	Extreme avoidance of situations where balance is needed (e.g., swings, seesaws, stairs); frequent experience of motion sickness	Rhythmic rocking behaviors, constantly high level of activity	1. Allow child to jump on small trampoline at regular intervals 2. Provide a rocking chair for rhythmic movement 3. Allow child to sit on texturized cushion 4. Encourage swinging, sliding, rolling, and spinning on playground and gym equipment

to other students. For example, a student might be placed beside an empty seat and desk or at the end of a table cluster.

Involve classmates. Because classmates often have a large impact on the sensory environment, involving them in managing the sensory stimuli makes sense. The volume of their sounds, the perfumes they wear, and their physical proximity often contribute to a sensory environment that the teacher can't control. Helping all students in the class develop empathy for the students with sensory integration difficulties and thereby managing the sensory level of the classroom will help students with ASD who have trouble with sensory integration. However, teachers also will need to, out of respect for the students, be sensitive to singling out any specific students with special needs. Rather, it can be helpful to introduce the exercise in Figure 1 to help every student develop a set of guidelines that they will want to abide by so as to have a comfortable classroom.

Teachers may want to establish a "home base" for students with ASD. The home base is a predesignated area that minimizes sources of stress (e.g., sensory, social) for the student with ASD. It's a predetermined place where ASD students can go whenever they are overwhelmed (e.g., experiencing sensory overload). The specific location of the home base varies depending on the level of resource provisions within the school and student needs and preferences. Examples of home bases include a quiet, "cozy" corner in the classroom; a resource room for students with ASD; the school counselor's or nurse's office; or a relaxation corner in the school library. Depending on students' needs, the home base may be a dim spot where the student can relax or a place where the student may engage in calming activities (e.g., reading a book, drawing) or an activity related to a special interest (e.g., Internet research for UFOs). Sending the student to the home base is not sending the student to time-out. Rather, it should be a place where the student can either request to go, or be directed to go whenever he or she feels or shows signs of stress. It is our experience that providing the choice(s) in writing (e.g., "John, I notice that you

Lesson Plan

Lesson Name: Creating a Sensory Neutral Classroom
Lesson Objectives:
1. To develop an awareness of the different sensory needs of each person.
2. To create a classroom that respects these needs.

Prior Knowledge: Participants have previously completed a lesson involving an
                    Internet search of the seven senses and are familiar with how
                    these senses impact them.
Lesson Duration: 120 minutes

Lesson Procedure:

Duration	Description	Materials
15 minutes	• The teacher revisits learning on seven senses. • The teacher introduces the concept of sensory overload using balloons of different sizes to illustrate how the capacities of each student are different.	• Material from previous lesson • Balloons of different sizes • Balloon pump
20 minutes	• Students are asked to reflect on those aspects of the classroom that may lead them to experience sensory overload. • Students anonymously fill in needs assessment.	• Handout on sensory overload • Needs assessment
50 minutes	• Divide class into workgroups comprised of 4 to 5 students. • Mix and distribute the handouts among workgroups. • As a work group, have students identify the sensory issues raised by the students in the class and brainstorm strategies for making the classroom a sensory-neutral zone.	• Butcher paper • Writing material
35 minutes	• Each workgroup presents its findings. • The teacher facilitates discussion on proposals for a sensory-neutral zone.	• Material to secure butcher paper to the wall or board

Figure 1. Lesson plan for creating a sensory-neutral classroom.

look a little stressed. Do you want to take a break in Mrs. Smith's room?"), as opposed to talking to the student, is helpful.

The home base also should not be a form of escape for the student. The student should be expected to return to the previous activity after he or she has calmed down. In some circumstances, students with ASD may take advantage of the home base and continually request to access it. In such cases, it may be helpful to restrict the number of times a day that the student with ASD can have access to the home base. It also is essential that an investigation be conducted in such cases into the reason(s) for the frequent requests for the home base. In some cases, the level of academic work in the class may be at a level that the student is unable to access. In others, the level of ambient noise may be too high. In still other cases, the activities at the home base may compete for the child's attention.

Socially Appropriate Coping Methods

Although the strategies mentioned above will reduce the probability of students with ASD being unduly stressed by the sensory environment, it's not possible to anticipate or control all situations. In those cases, the following strategies may help.

Teach the student when to ask for a break. Most students with ASD who are gifted are able to recognize when they are feeling calm and comfortable, and when they are feeling very stressed and overwhelmed. However, many have difficulties recognizing the gradation between the calm and stressed states. It may be helpful to introduce a five- or seven-point stress thermometer (see Figure 2) to help them recognize and monitor how they feel through the day. As many students with ASD may have trouble understanding the rationale behind why they have to record stress, some find it helpful to have it introduced in the form of a worksheet (see Figure 3). Once the student is able to monitor stress, he or she can be taught to request a break when his or her stress rating exceeds a certain level.

Teach the student how to relax. Many students who find certain environments stressful may be able to apply relaxation strategies

5	Being trapped in an elevator with a baby who does not stop crying
4	Sitting in the classroom with construction going on downstairs
3	Mrs. Chan shouting at the class when we are noisy
2	Flag raising ceremony in the morning
1	Playing games at the computer

Instructions: Taking "5" as a situation that is extremely stressful, "3" as a situation that is somewhat stressful, and "1" that is a situation where you will be completely relaxed, please write in examples of situations that will lead you to feel these levels of stress.

Figure 2. Stress meter.

to reduce their stress. One common strategy is to have the student with ASD take a deep breath, clench his fist, and then count from 1 to 10. Another strategy involves teaching the student with ASD to employ her visual strengths and to build a picture in her mind of a preferred relaxing area. When teaching students with ASD, it is important to remember that places that teachers may consider relaxing (e.g., beach vacation scenes) may not be calming to a student. One similar strategy is to have students participate in engaging activities that are of interest to them. For example, one student found it relaxing to write out all of the prime numbers. Others may find it helpful to engage in activities such as reading or Internet research on a topic of interest.

Tips for Managing Stressful Situations
    Following are strategies that have been found helpful in managing crisis situations related to sensory overload.

Understanding Stress

Stress is what you feel when you have to handle more than you are used to. When you are stressed, your body responds as though you are in danger. Some stress is normal and even useful. It can help if you need to work hard or react quickly. For example, it can help you win a race or finish an important job on time. But if stress happens too often or lasts too long, it can have bad effects.

It is important to understand about stress in order to control it.

Stress can be recognized from how our *body reacts* to it. Stress warning signs can help us understand our level of stress. Here are some warning signs of stress:

- increased heartbeat,
- breathing faster,
- dry mouth,
- shoulder muscles tighten up, and
- clenched fist.

Stress is also a feeling or an *emotion*. One way of thinking about stress is to think of you being a thermometer. When you are feeling very stressed, the mercury level is very high and when you are not stressed, the level is low. We call this a stress thermometer.

People also *act* certain ways when they get stressed. For example, some people bite their nails. Others may yell at others. What are some things that you do when you get stressed?

Figure 3. Understanding stress.

Stay calm and communicate in writing. In contrast to what often works with gifted kids, "talking things through" is typically not a useful problem-solving strategy with gifted students with ASD in light of the difficulties in auditory processing and in understanding social situations that some experience. In contrast, it has a tendency to heighten the level of sensory stimulation (humans have a tendency to speak louder, faster, and in a higher pitch when they are stressed) and further stress the student. Instead, keeping one's voice steady and emotionally neutral (however difficult it may be) and using a written medium to communicate with the student may be more effective. E-mails, cell phone text messages, or handwritten notes all are useful alternatives because they remove the ambiguity of the social interaction and allow the child to operate in his or her preferred modality (e.g., visual). Written communication also helps the teacher determine the specific message that needs to be delivered. This writing process also increases the level of clarity in communication.

Summary

In this section, the nature of sensory integration difficulties among gifted students with ASD has been highlighted. To help avoid the occurrence of crisis situations that may arise from their being unable to manage the sensory environment, strategies have been proposed that may be implemented by teachers, parents, or the student with ASD. Interventions and strategies that can be implemented when the student with ASD enters a crisis situation also have been presented. In its essence, the best method of supporting students with ASD is to understand the difficulties they experience and to equip the students and their teacher, parents, and classmates with an awareness of these difficulties and options when they occur.

Coping With Planning and Organization Difficulties

Gifted children with ASD typically have a great capacity to generate and engage in advanced, complex, and original thinking in one or more domains, but often experience extreme difficulties with organization and planning. In some cases, these difficulties are profound and may shock teachers who are unprepared for them. When stacked together with difficulties in sequencing and generalizing, this discrepancy in particular is one that keeps some gifted students with ASD out of the most challenging classes because they are not able to cope with the organizational demands of such classrooms. However, if teachers put in a little extra work, it is possible to support students with these difficulties. Therefore, in order to ensure optimal educational placements and to support their talent development, teachers must be prepared to collaborate with parents and other specialists to accommodate these deficits and teach the students how to cope. This section begins by examining how to help draw the attention of students with ASD to important detail and to increase their efficiency of work. A strategy is suggested for helping ASD students better cope with transitions in location and time. Finally, strategies for helping students with ASD follow-through on assignments and projects are described.

Increasing Organization and Efficiency: Visual Structure

As a result of difficulties in auditory processing, attention, planning, and organization, some ASD students gloss over important details or work very slowly. Research suggests that the provision of visual structure helps improve the level of organization and the speed of processing for these students. Visual structure is defined as ways in which work to be done is made clearer via the provision of visual instructions, visual clarity, and visual organization (Mesibov, Shea, & Schopler, 2004). Visual supports are consistent with the visual learning style that is preferred by many individuals with ASD and circumvent auditory processing difficulties or periods of inattention.

Visual instructions and reminders. Instead of verbal instructions, many students with ASD benefit from written instructions (e.g., writing on the chalkboard or on a piece of paper). Likewise, written reminders can be provided. Some students benefit from written reminders posted on their desks for requesting a break when they are feeling overstimulated or stressed. In such cases, the teacher need not verbally remind the students (which is frequently perceived as nagging and may lead to overstimulation) and can simply point or tap on the written reminder.

Visual clarity. Another way to help increase the speed of processing is to draw students' attention to the pertinent aspects of the tasks at hand. This may take the form of simply coloring or highlighting details and other instructions. This strategy may benefit other twice-exceptional students as well, such as those with Attention Deficit Hyperactivity Disorder (ADHD).

Visual organization. One common complaint made by teachers about students with ASD is their level of messiness and/or disorganization. Although this difficulty does not always directly impact their ability to complete their work, it frequently slows them down. The following are some suggestions for helping organize students with ASD:

- limit materials (e.g., having only one spare pen, bringing only books that are needed);
- organize materials into containers (e.g., labeled clear zipper bags); and
- segment materials (e.g., using box pencil cases with segmented compartments to store supplies).

Assistive technology, or the use of computer-based resources designed to aid individuals with disabilities, should be maximized to help gifted students with ASD predict and respond appropriately to common sequences and routine changes. Software (see Resources for suggestions) is available to help clarify schedules and routines and organize common tasks and assignments. In addition, communicating via e-mail is an easier means for students with ASD to initiate social contacts, and its use can promote independence and initiative (Klin, Volkmar, & Sparrow, 2000).

Managing Transitions: Individualized Schedules

Gifted students with ASD have difficulty with sequencing events. For example, one very bright adult with ASD may try to schedule grocery shopping and banking en route to a meeting that starts in 15 minutes. It may be due to this difficulty in sequencing that many people with ASD find it difficult to cope with changes to their schedules. Visuals such as schedules are widely recommended to help ASD students predict and respond appropriately to common sequences of events and to routine change. Schedules are visual cues that indicate what activities will occur and in what sequence (Mesibov et al., 2004). Although schedules are common in all education settings (particularly in high schools), many gifted students with ASD need a schedule that is individualized to meet their needs. Several considerations for making the most of individualized schedules follow (see Mesibov et al., 2004, for a broader discussion).

Schedule length. The length of a schedule refers to the duration of time within the day for which the schedule provides information. Formats range from simply providing what activity occurs next in a sequence, to a morning, a half-day, and a full-day schedule. Shorter schedules may be appropriate in cases when information for the entire day isn't easily determined or when the schedule is subject to frequent changes (such as in pull-out classrooms or seminar format classes).

Schedule format. It is essential to consider the format that the individualized schedule will take. In the case of gifted students with ASD, formats include a schedule that is mounted on the wall or on a clipboard, written in the student's daily planner, or entered into a cell phone or personal digital assistant (PDA). In every case, the need for an age-appropriate schedule (which determines its social acceptability) needs to be weighed against the ease of student access (which increases the probability of the schedule being used).

Time. One important consideration is whether to include the time when the student is expected to be in a certain place and/or participating in a specific activity. This consideration frequently depends, in turn, upon two factors: the probability of the activity occurring within the stipulated period, and the degree to which a student can cope with variations in the starting and ending time of an activity.

Use of cues. Just because children have a schedule doesn't mean they'll use it! Cues such as the school bell, a half-hourly chime set on the digital watch, or a verbal or written instruction are common cues used to remind students to check the schedule. More often than not, students with ASD employ a combination of these cues to check their schedule. The school bell can be an especially important cue for checking a schedule, particularly for gifted students with ASD attending schools where there is an expectation that they are able to transition between locations independently.

Management of the schedule. Another consideration is when and how to manipulate the schedule, if necessary. This issue is particularly pertinent for students who are able to read and understand the items of a schedule but who may frequently miss, overlook, or skip items in a list. For gifted students with ASD, this may take the form of check boxes or striking through completed tasks. Having the students mark out an item that they have read is helpful as it will be visually evident which item they will need to refer to next. Furthermore, it may be helpful for students with visual scanning and organizational difficulties to adopt a "read-check-do" routine where they read the line on the schedule, check or cross it off, and then do it. This prevents a situation whereby the student follows through with an item but forgets to check it off, only to return to a list of scheduled items that he or she needs to visually scan before figuring out where to go next.

Helping students cope with change. A related issue is the degree to which the student manages schedule changes in a flexible fashion. Secondary students in particular may face substantial schedule changes and transitions if they're participating in an accelerated or advanced program. Although some students with ASD handle changes without a problem, others may find such changes particularly stressful and anxiety provoking. Sometimes, it's this inability to cope with change that keeps a child from full participation in the most challenging courses or programs. Students who have difficulties with change can be supported by introducing change as a regular component.

Figure 4 depicts the individualized schedule of a gifted boy with ASD who has difficulties managing changes to his schedule. To help him with this issue, the school team met and decided to introduce change as a regular feature of his schedule (depicted as a "Surprise!"). To begin, the schedule change should be something positive (e.g., Martin will get to spend 30 minutes surfing the Internet or conducting research on his favorite topic). Once Martin is accustomed to positive changes, the planned changes

Martin's Timetable

Time	Description	Person	Location
7:45 a.m.	Physical Education: • Change clothes in boy's bathroom • **Remember to bring your shorts and T-shirt!**	Mr. Clendon	Gym
8:30 a.m.	English: • Get textbook from locker	Mrs. Gopal	134 Hall H
9:15 a.m.	Math: • Mr. Sweetser will be in class	Miss Gordon	139 Hall H
10 a.m.	Spanish: • Pick up book from Mr. Rodriguez	Mr. Rodriguez	88 Hall G
11:15 a.m.	Resource Room: • Bring notebook	Mr. Sweetser	Annex B across from music room
11:45 a.m.	Lunch	Mr. Sweetser	Annex B across from music room
12:15 p.m.	Band	~~Mrs. Richardson~~ Relief Teacher	~~Music Room~~ Class P51
1 p.m.	Science	Mrs. Benjamin	136 Hall H
1:45 p.m.	Seminar **Surprise!**	Mrs. Hani	Media Center
3:30 p.m.	Go Home: • Stop at locker first to get English book • Take bus B near the corner		Left corner in front of building

Figure 4. Individualized schedule for Martin, a gifted boy with ASD in middle school receiving itinerant teacher support.

can be neutral in nature (e.g., doing homework). Finally, changes introduced to Martin can be extended to include not only positive and neutral events, but also less preferred events (e.g., a change in teacher or room location). By introducing schedule changes in this way, students can learn that coping effectively with change is a skill that needs to be developed and they will build their capacity to deal with unexpected, negative change.

Following Through Tasks and Projects: Work Systems

Many gifted ASD students don't lack the skill set to accomplish a task but rather lack a strategy to systematically approach the task at hand. Mesibov and colleagues (2004) proposed that the best way to support students with difficulties approaching the task is to introduce a work system for every task in which the student engages. Furthermore, each work system needs to provide answers to the following questions:

- What work am I to do?
- How much do I have to do?
- When does it end, and how do I know that I am making progress?
- What comes next?

Applications of the work system. Work systems have wide applications and may be applied in virtually all aspects of the school environment, but only to the extent that the student needs them. Figures 5–8 depict work systems for Martin from the previous example (Figure 4) across a few contexts. A visual contrast of these three work systems (see Table 3) helps illustrate that despite their varied uses, each work system answers each of the four questions posed previously. Furthermore, it should be noted that a work system is likely to be helpful not only for students with ASD but for all students (and particularly for students with developmental coordination disorder and ADHD).

Individualize the work system. As with the case of individualized schedules, work systems need to be individualized. First, the form that the work system takes needs to be considered. Examples include checklists (e.g., Figures 5 and 6) or templates (e.g., Figures 7 and 8). These may in turn be mounted on the table, in the student daily planner, or posted within the student's personal digital assistant or cell phone.

Table 3
Comparison of Work Systems

	Class-Based Group Project	Homework	Studying for Exams
What work?	Each line beside a check box indicates what needs to be done.	Each line beside a check box indicates what needs to be done.	Each line under the header "topic" indicates the topic to be reviewed.
How much work?	The number of check boxes indicates how many tasks need to be completed.	The number of check boxes indicates how many tasks need to be completed.	The total number of topics to be reviewed indicates the quantity of work to be done.
Concept of progress and finishing	When all the boxes are checked, the tasks are finished.	When all the boxes are checked, the tasks are finished.	Progress is noted as the student indicates the date that the topic was reviewed.
What comes next?	The student is prompted to check his or her schedule.	The student is prompted to check his or her schedule.	The student is prompted to try a trial math exam paper.

Project Work With Kirsten, Juan, & DeShawn: Meeting 1

❑   Read social story: *Working With My Classmates for a Group Project.*

❑   Read instructions on handout and discuss topic for group project.

Write chosen topic here: _____

❑   Decide on roles in this project (refer to second page of handout for suggested roles that each member can take).

Write chosen role here: _____

❑   Identify my task and set deadlines for each part of the task (please fill in Worksheet: Planning for Project Work).

Remember: It's OK to ask my classmates for their opinion on my plans.

❑   Set a date to meet again (write the meeting date into my planner).

❑   Check my schedule (if there is enough time, read in the Media Center).

READ-CHECK-DO

Figure 5. Work system for a class-based group project.

Homework to Complete
❏   English—Read pages 26 to 32 from "Greek Myths"
❏   Math—Complete odd problems on pages 218–219 and problems on page 225
❏   Science—Internet research (follow steps on handout)
❏   Take a 30-minute break
❏   Check my schedule

Figure 6. Work system for homework.

Subject Review Planner		
Subject: Social Studies		
Topic for Review	**Planned Completion Date**	**Date Completed**
1 Vocabulary	Feb. 12	
2 Events leading up to Revolutionary War	Feb. 13	
3 Major victories and turning points in the war	Feb. 14	
4 Reasons colonists won the war	Feb. 15	
5		
6		
7		
When I am finished: Take the practice quiz		

Figure 7. Work system for test study.

Planning for Project Work	
Task Description	**Deadline**
1. Make a list of all activities that need to be done to complete the project.	March 16
2. Check with Mr. Sweetser to see if I need to add anything.	March 17
3. Decide when each task on the list should be done (set a due date) and make a list of materials I will need to do each thing.	March 19
4. Start working on first task	March 26

Figure 8. Work system for project work.

Summary

Despite their intellectual strengths, many gifted students with ASD continue to experience planning and organization difficulties that may hinder them from achieving their full potential. In this section, individualized schedules, work systems, and visual structures have been described. When these interventions are implemented in a way to support their difficulties, gifted students with ASD are more likely to achieve their potential.

Managing Special Interests

Gifted children with and without ASD often have special interests. We frequently refer to them as passions or even obsessions, but there is a distinct quality between the special interests of gifted children with and without the disorder. Attwood (2007) observed three types of special interests among people with ASD:

- objects (e.g., trains, dinosaurs),
- topics (e.g., transportation, sports, death, military history, pretense, brands, schedules), and
- people (e.g., movie stars, politicians, classmates).

Special interests among gifted children with ASD often serve the purposes of overcoming anxiety, providing pleasure and relaxation, achieving coherence, understanding the physical world, creating an alternative world, developing a sense of identity, occupying time, facilitating conversation, and indicating intelligence (Attwood, 2007). Parents and educators often have found it very difficult and frequently unhelpful to suppress or change the interest of a person with ASD. Rather, special interests should be treated as latent talents that need to be managed instead of extinguished. In a way, this is consistent with how passions are viewed among gifted children where passions are topics or things the child has become captivated with and has a strong desire to learn more about. It's this "falling in love with an idea" that's commonly seen among highly intelligent or creative people.

Harnessing Special Interests

The strong intrinsic value of these special interests for gifted students with ASD makes it an important tool for teachers to utilize. The following are some ideas.

Motivational tool. Special interests may be used to motivate or reward gifted ASD students. For example, a primary student with a special interest in Alexander the Great may be given the task of researching how far the commander traveled in pursuit of his conquests to engage the student in a math topic that may otherwise be of little interest to him or her. Similarly, this same student may be allowed time to complete Wikipedia entries on Alexander the Great following the satisfactory completion of required work.

Relaxation aid. As previously mentioned, engagement in a special interest may be used as a strategy for stress management. For example, one gifted ASD student found that counting the number of prime numbers between a range of numbers was an effective tool for alleviating stress. Essentially, special interests can be used as distracters, allowing students to relax while engaging in a preferred activity.

Tool for talent and career development. When appropriate, the special interests of the student may be developed further, just as talent development is a priority for all gifted children. For instance, one young boy had his interest in dinosaurs expanded to that of paleontology. Ultimately, it is hoped that these special interests of the gifted student with ASD may be honed to a level of strength that provides a form of employment for the student (e.g., academic research).

Strategy for connecting with others. Although most people with ASD find it difficult to interact with others in social settings, many find it much easier to interact with others in settings that are familiar (i.e., in which they have a special interest). Gifted students with ASD who are able to excel in their chosen fields of interest may become more confident in interacting with others. For example, one bright young man not only found friends, but also a girlfriend, in a club that brought people with similar interests together.

Strategies for Managing Special Interests

Although it is ideal to utilize a special interest to support a gifted student with ASD, there may be times when a special interest negatively impacts the educational setting. Even under such circumstances, it should be emphasized that topics of special interest rarely are inappropriate. Rather, it is frequently the time, place, audience, or intensity of the activity that is inappropriate. Therefore, the challenge for teachers, parents, and other school professionals is the appropriate *management* rather than the removal of the special interest (which usually proves futile). Specifying when to engage in a special interest activity respects a student's interest while specifying the boundaries within which the special interest can take place. Similarly, when a special interest is problematic, the time, place, people, duration, and frequency of engagement in the special interest must be structured. In addition, it is recommended that time for the special interest is incorporated into the student's individualized schedule.

Still, there may be unusual circumstances when the content or activity associated with a special interest is inappropriate (e.g., starting fires, removing clothes). In such circumstances, social stories and comic strip conversations (Gray, 1994, 1998) help students understand why such topics are inappropriate. Wherever possible, such interests need to be modified to a form that is more acceptable. Furthermore, Attwood (2007) proposed helping the student develop another interest that replaces the inappropriate one.

Summary

Special interests are one unique aspect of some gifted students with ASD. In most cases, the special interest of the student represents a latent talent with enormous potential for development and a very powerful motivator. Although this may mean a shift in mindset for parents and teachers, it is important for teaching any gifted student and essential for helping gifted students with ASD learn.

Developing Social Competence

A key characteristic of children with ASD is poor social communication. They typically have great difficulty identifying and understanding the thoughts and feelings of others. Their sensory integration difficulties, slow auditory processing, and poor speech pragmatics work together to create huge barriers to forming social connections and developing age-appropriate social behaviors. This is a key difference between gifted children with and without the disorder. As a group, gifted children tend to be advanced in their social and emotional development when compared to their age peers (Neihart et al., 2002), but the gap between cognitive and social abilities is much greater in gifted children with ASD. This discrepancy may present the greatest challenge for the provision of appropriate educational services for gifted children with ASD, for although they may be ready for the intellectual challenge of gifted programs and advanced classes, they are frequently unable to handle the social demands of such environments without considerable support.

Although there are few controlled clinical studies to confirm the effectiveness of many interventions, there is wide consensus that students can improve their social skills with training so that they can fully participate in programming for gifted students (Bernad-Ripoli, 2007; Bock, 2007; Sansosti, Powell-Smith, & Kincaid, 2004). However, it is crucial that the training take into account the child's unique profile of strengths and weaknesses.

It is usually of little benefit to explain to gifted students with ASD what they need to change. Even if they understand what is communicated and can verbalize what is appropriate, they are unlikely to be able to convert that knowledge into action (Atwood, 2007; Klin et al., 2000; Mesibov, 1984). As a result, others may view them as uncaring, insensitive, tactless, or even cruel, but nothing could be further from the truth. So, one might determine that the first intervention is to talk less. When auditory instructions are given, they should be limited to one action at a time and be as literal and as bluntly explicit as possible.

These students often are strong visual thinkers and *need to see*, rather than hear, what it is expected of them. Make everything as visual as possible—schedules, instructions, lectures, homework, and group discussions. Videos, mirrors, digital cameras, and social stories are recommended for teaching social skills. Children with ASD need an active, direct, and structured approach. They need to see, say, and do. In this fashion, they can learn to recognize the feeling states of others and label their own feelings accurately. They can work to improve the match between their facial expression, intonation, and body language with their feeling states. They can improve the accuracy of their interpretations of others' emotions and nonverbal language. They can develop social problem-solving skills.

Social Stories

One intervention for developing social competence that is widely popular and has been demonstrated in some empirical studies (Sansosti et al., 2004) to be effective is social stories. A social story (Gray, 1994, 1998; Gray & Garand, 1993) is a brief narrative that helps people make sense of social situations. In just four to eight sentences, a social story describes the norms of behavior in a specific social situation, the perspectives of others, and specific steps for age-appropriate interaction. In other words, social stories teach the appropriate behavioral response for a social encounter. They are written only after a detailed assessment of the child's behavioral strengths and weaknesses.

Gray (1994, 1998) is credited with the development of the social story as a communication intervention. She proposed four steps in the intervention:
1. identify a specific social situation;
2. identify the salient features of the situation (e.g., who, what, where, how long) and obtain a baseline of the child's strengths and weaknesses;

3. share the data with parents, teachers, and the student; and
4. write the social story.

Writing a social story. Social stories include four types of sentences. *Descriptive* sentences describe the setting. They tell what happens, where, and why. *Perspective* sentences explain the thoughts and feelings of others in the situation. They describe internal processes. *Directive* sentences explain the norm behavior—the appropriate response, or they may identify who will help the child and how they will help. Because children with ASD typically are quite literal in their understanding, it is recommended that directive sentences begin with "I will try to . . ." or "I will work on . . ." rather than "I will . . ." *Affirmative* sentences are statements about the shared beliefs or values of a culture. Gray (1994) originally suggested a ratio of two to five descriptive, perspective, and affirmative sentences for every directive sentence, but the ratio has never been empirically challenged or validated. What's important is that the social story emphasizes explaining more than directing.

Following are three examples of social stories. The first was written for a gifted, 13-year-old student with ASD who would remove her shirt in school when she was too hot. The second example was written for an adolescent boy who didn't brush his teeth. Because all children with ASD will face situations when they don't know what to do, they, their parents, and school personnel should agree on a simple plan for what they are to do when they don't know what to do. The third example is a social story that taught one child what to do in such situations.

Example 1

Too Hot

Sometimes I feel hot and uncomfortable indoors. It's not OK to take my clothes off. My friends want me to keep my clothes on. I can ask to open a window or go outside. I will try to ask to open a window or go outside when I feel too hot.

Example 2

Bad Breath

My breath smells bad when I don't brush my teeth. People at school don't like to smell bad breath. I can brush my teeth every morning. Toothpaste stops the bad smell. I can brush my teeth with toothpaste. I will try to remember to brush my teeth every morning.

Example 3

I Don't Know What to Do

Sometimes at school I don't know what to do. That's OK. I will take two deep breaths and tell myself it's OK. I can ask _____ to help me. I can say, "I don't understand what to do." _____ will tell me and I will try to listen. I will work on asking for help when I don't know what to do.

Using a social story. The first step is to consider the child's comprehension, reading level, and interests. Selecting an approach for implementation depends on the needs and abilities of the child in question (Sansosti et al., 2004). Social stories can be:
- read independently or by a caregiver or teacher,
- presented orally,
- presented via a computer program, or
- videotaped.

Summary

Developing social communication is an often neglected but essential component of talent development with gifted children with ASD. As a result of their deficits in auditory information processing, sensory integration, and poor speech pragmatics, gifted children with ASD face huge social challenges. This section has explained how visual supports are pivotal to developing social communication and has demonstrated how social stories can be written and implemented to build better functional communication skills.

A common problem for gifted children with ASD is that classes for gifted students have greater social complexity than that of the regular classroom. Is it better for these children to remain in the regular classroom where they feel safer and more secure but not adequately challenged, or is it possible to provide sufficient support for them to participate in programming for gifted children? Concerns about educational placement often become a major issue during the transition between elementary and secondary school and secondary school and college, because increased support is sometimes needed for the child to succeed at the next level. Parents, in particular, may be a reluctant to suddenly utilize special education services in middle or high school because to do so seems a regressive step.

However, most gifted students with ASD will need considerable emotional, social, and instructional support to be successful at the secondary level because the social milieu is very complex. In advanced classes or gifted programs, the pace will be faster, the students generally more socially sophisticated (and perhaps less tolerant of classmates whose behavior is immature), and the organization and time management demands much greater than regular classes.

Increased supports also will be necessary to ensure optimal functioning. Teachers and parents must be proactive in planning for these transitions. Without preplanning and increasing support, even gifted students with ASD who did very well in elementary school are likely to deteriorate behaviorally, emotionally, and academically at home and/or at school following the transition. "Once the student's difficulties increase, a great deal of effort is often required to stabilize the situation, with significant increases in the amount of supports being needed in order to do so" (Adreon & Stella, 2000, p. 1). Some of the challenges a gifted ASD student may face in high school are described in this parent's personal account:

> We had to be ever vigilant mainly in situations that had to do with group work or very nonstructured learning assignments. . . . The rigidity of ASD also becomes problematic when a student is asked to write a paper on something that is a known failure (e.g., he would not "waste his time" writing a paper on the League of Nations). He would not write papers dealing with science fiction or fantasy because these things could not possibly have happened. (Reitschel, 2000, p. 451)

Most importantly, an agreed upon "I need help" code the student can use with all adults at school should be established. When school personnel see the code, they know to provide the student with a means of de-stressing by going with the student to a quiet area where he or she can use his or her preferred calming strategies (e.g., listening to music for a few minutes, having a back massage, doing joint compressions). All staff members who have contact with the student should be able to demonstrate the plan that is to be followed when there are behavioral problems. Before school starts, and occasionally throughout the school year, have the student practice having a problem and using the agreed upon "I need help" signal.

Children with ASD should be evaluated by an occupational therapist trained in sensory integration therapy to determine the nature and severity of the student's sensory integration difficulties. Once the nature of these difficulties is known, it is relatively easy to accommodate such students in the classroom. For instance, items that help the child avert sensory overload should be readily available (e.g., sunglasses, earplugs, a weighted vest, aromatherapy lotion, squeeze balls). Scheduling downtime for the student to reduce high arousal states (often about every 2 hours for elementary students) also is advisable.

Transitions and Change

Students with ASD typically have trouble with even the smallest changes in routine. Elementary students in particular may not be able to learn in a gifted pull-out class if the schedule and types of activities change every week. Because children with ASD don't follow auditory directions well, unexpected changes are often a significant stressor and can cause meltdowns. Fire drills, substitute teachers, special assemblies, and other changes in schedule will increase their anxiety. Having a buddy system in place for these less common situations can facilitate smooth transitions.

When faced with new, upcoming situations like competitions, field trips, or meeting new people, it can be helpful to write social stories ahead of time. Even if the child doesn't learn the story, just having it in hand can sometimes go a long way in reducing anxiety.

Some gifted ASD students may do fine in a regular classroom situation, but have considerable difficulty with less structured times like recess, bus rides, lunch, PE, the bathroom, and before- and afterschool activities. The social demands of these situations are more complex and sensory stimuli are increased, augmenting the chances that the student will behave inappropriately.

Arranging for an escort, increased supervision, or options to be elsewhere at these times can help alleviate these issues. Such necessary adaptations also should be listed in the child's IEP or 504 plan, including those associated with lunch, bathroom breaks, recess, and bus rides.

Group Work

It is crucial that gifted students with ASD be introduced to learning groups early, no later than upper elementary school, so they have ample opportunity to learn effective coping skills before they enter the more complicated social milieu of secondary school. When students are working in groups, students with ASD should be placed with a supportive group of peers, or have at least one peer who is sensitive to their needs and willing to assist them. In addition, students with ASD should be allowed to work with the same group or team all year so that they will be more likely to take intellectual and social risks.

Teasing or bullying never should be tolerated, and steps should be taken to reduce the chances of a student being victimized (e.g., preferential seating, supervision at specified times, alternative placements for lunch or breaks, use of an escort, or different times for moving from one place to another). Using a buddy system or teaming the student with a sensitive gifted peer to increase the ASD student's sense of safety and security also is recommended.

Postsecondary Planning

Like other twice-exceptional students, gifted students with ASD will require advance planning time and assistance to locate postsecondary options that provide support for students with social disabilities. It's unlikely that they will have trouble with the academic aspects of college life. Instead, time management, organizational skills, and relationships with faculty and peers are likely to be the issues that will challenge them the most (Reis,

McGuire, & Neu, 2000; Reis & Neu, 1994). Although assistive technology is available at virtually all colleges now, only a few offer supports like "quiet dorms." Requesting a private room also is an option. If a high school student is seeing a therapist, it is a good idea to get the names of counselors who are knowledgeable about the disorder at the college counseling center or at a mental health center near the university the student will be attending. Similarly, other specialists whom the student is meeting with regularly (e.g., psychiatrists, occupational therapists, speech and language specialists) should be consulted to determine what supports will need to be in place to maximize chances for success in college (Mangrum, Strichart, & Latimer, 1997; Rietschel, 2000; Schissel, 1999; Sclafani & Lynch, 1995).

As with other transitions, gifted students with ASD benefit a great deal by practicing going to college in small steps. Participation in summer residential programs with good emotional supports is beneficial, provided the student understands his disorder and has demonstrated an ability to self-advocate. Attending a community college closer to home during the first year or two may be a useful intermediate step, provided an appropriate level of academic challenge is available. Prior to enrollment, students should visit with the disability coordinator at state schools or the dean of students at private schools to communicate their specific needs. It's recommended (Schissel, 1999) that students bring these officials a brief written explanation of ASD and of their own personal learning profile.

Conclusion

Gifted students with autism spectrum disorders have serious social communication deficits that may compromise their high achievement if they do not receive accurate diagnosis and appropriate supports. The most common difficulties they face are sensory overload, poor auditory processing, and an inability to infer the internal states of others. As a result of their combined difficulties with fine motor and auditory processing speed, some gifted students with ASD understandably choose to resist tasks that involve both because they find them so frustrating. Teachers and parents who don't appreciate their profile of strengths and weaknesses may wrongly conclude that these students are rigid, stubborn, lazy, or defiant.

Following a comprehensive assessment designed to capture their unique profile of abilities, the first step in effective instruction is educating teachers about this exceptionality. Teachers who don't understand what is going on with these children may wonder, "How can a child so bright fail to understand the simplest social behaviors?" Or, the bizarre behavior of a gifted child with ASD may reinforce some teacher's misguided assumptions that gifted students are social misfits: "Some kids are just too smart for their own good." Worse, people may assume the child is manipulative, or is using his intelligence to find creative ways to be oppositional and create havoc in the classroom.

Although there are few controlled clinical studies to confirm the effectiveness of many interventions (Bock, 2007; Sansosti & Powell-Smith, 2006; Sansosti et al., 2004), there is wide consensus that students can learn social skills and manage their sensory sensitivities so effectively that they can fully participate in their school's gifted program. Sensory integration therapy is effective in improving motor and sensory synchronicity, and in developing individualized strategies for affect regulation. Social stories, assistive technology, and visual supports capitalize on the strong visual-spatial skills of these learners to help them establish routines for handling social situations, novelty, and common tasks or assignments.

It is important to remember that although many gifted students with the disorder will be able to attend classes for gifted students when these supports are in place, there are some gifted children with ASD who need a level of support services that precludes them from participating in their school's gifted program, at least for a time. There are cases, too, where gifted children with ASD are better served in private or residential programs than in public schools. In those cases, it is still imperative that their intellectual needs be met. The healthy adjustment of gifted students is compromised when they lack appropriate challenge in the curriculum and when they have few opportunities to learn with people who share their interests and abilities (Gross, 1993; Neihart et al., 2002)

It will be necessary to provide additional training for the gifted teacher, who may understand giftedness, but may not be familiar with the impact ASD has on the child's academic, emotional, and social functioning. Educational planning should include specialists (e.g., augmentative communication specialist, resource teacher, assistive technology specialist, occupational therapist, behavior specialist) to consult with teachers and parents and plan effective strategies for enhancing social communication and for managing behaviors. Professionals acquainted with the needs and behaviors of gifted children should take a careful, systematic approach to assessing a gifted student's social withdrawal, alleged boredom, and sensitivity before attributing their behaviors to a need for more a more stimulating environment.

In summary, the following checklist of broad strategies is recommended to guide schools and families as they accommodate the unusual profile of gifted children with ASD and develop supports and strategies to develop their talents:

Check all that apply:

- ❏ A simple plan has been established with the child regarding what to do when he or she doesn't know what to do.
- ❏ The same plan can be implemented schoolwide.
- ❏ Time is allotted during the school day for the child's special interests.
- ❏ An appropriate level of challenge is provided, especially in the child's areas of strength.
- ❏ Information is presented visually to the greatest extent possible (e.g., schedules, instructions, lectures, outlines, deadlines, main ideas, etc).
- ❏ Persistence to completion and a willingness to work more slowly than gifted classmates is positively reinforced.
- ❏ Timed tasks are avoided.
- ❏ Planning occurs ahead of time for special events, and the child is allowed extra options for reducing sensory overload.
- ❏ Whenever possible, additional time for completing assignments is granted.
- ❏ There are frequent checks for understanding and it is never assumed that the child's comprehension matches his or her verbal or computation ability.
- ❏ Teasing and bullying are monitored closely and interventions are implemented immediately when such behavior is observed.
- ❏ There is resistance to conclude that the child is careless, lazy, or defiant.

Books

Grandin, T. (2006). *Thinking in pictures: My life with autism.* New York: Vintage Books.

Haddon, M. (2004). *The curious incident of the dog in the night-time.* New York: Vintage on Amazon.

Hodgdon, L. (1996). *Visual strategies for improving communication. Volume 1: Practical supports for home and school.* Troy, MI: QuirkRoberts.

Kranowitz, C. (2006). *The out-of-sync child: Recognizing and coping with sensory integration dysfunction* (Rev. ed.). New York: Perigee Books.

Kurcinka, M. S. (2006). *Raising your spirited child: A guide for parents whose child is more intense, sensitive, perceptive, persistent, and energetic* (Rev. ed.). New York: Harper Perennial.

Myles, B. S., & Southwick, J. (1999). *Asperger syndrome and difficult moments: Practical solutions for tantrums, rage, and meltdowns.* Shawnee Mission, KS: Autism Asperger Publishing Company.

Tammet, D. (2006). *Born on a blue day.* New York: Simon & Schuster.

Web Sites

Autism Society of America
http://www.autism-society.org/site/PageServer
This site offers downloadable information packets.

OASIS—Online Asperger Syndrome Information and Support
http://www.udel.edu/bkirby/asperger
In addition to offering an excellent library of papers and articles, information, and resources, this Web site lists upcoming events and publications about ASD and hosts two listservs for people who wish to dialogue with parents, clinicians, educators, and individuals with disabilities.

TEACCH Autism Program
http://www.teacch.com
This is the official Web site of the training and research program in autism at the University of North Carolina's Department of Psychiatry. Internationally recognized as one of the leaders in training and research, this program's Web site is a treasure trove of information about teaching kits for home and school, training videos, scientific papers and books, and training programs for people with ASD.

Software

Picture Exchange Communication System (PECS)
http://www.pecs.com
This is the official Web site of one of the most well-established visual communication systems, PECS, which is an augmentative communication system that helps children with ASD develop more functional communication. Software is available with printable pictures for more than 2,000 words.

Social Skill Builder
http://www.socialskillbuilder.com
This is a series of five computer software programs designed to help children between the ages of 5–15 develop appropriate social communication skills. Each program includes five levels that use video clips with spoken and written language. A big plus includes the many features that allow for customization to a child's specific needs.

References

Adreon, D., & Stella, J. L. (2000, Winter). Transitioning AS students to middle and high school. *The Source, 1,* 4–5, 9.

Assouline, S. G., Foley Nicpon, M., Colangelo, N., & O'Brien, M. (2007). *The paradox of giftedness and autism: Packet of information for professionals.* Iowa City: The University of Iowa, The Connie Belin & Jacqueline N. Blank International Center for Gifted Education and Talent Development. Retrieved from http://www.education.uiowa.edu/belinblank/clinic/pip.pdf

Attwood, T. (2007). *The complete guide to Asperger's syndrome.* London: Jessica Kingsley.

Bernad-Ripoli, S. (2007). Using a self-as-model video with social stories to help a child with Asperger syndrome understand emotions. *Focus on Autism and Other Developmental Disabilities, 22,* 100–106.

Bock, M. A. (2007). The impact of social-behavioral learning strategy training on the social interaction skills of four students with Asperger syndrome. *Focus on Autism and Other Developmental Disabilities, 22,* 88–95.

Capps, S. C., & Gere, D. (1999, November). *Sensory sensitivities of gifted children.* Paper presented at the annual convention of the National Association for Gifted Children, Albuquerque, NM.

Centers for Disease Control and Prevention. (2007). *Prevalence of autism spectrum disorders: Autism and developmental disabilities monitoring network, 14 sites, United States, 2002.* Retrieved August 10, 2008, from http://www.cdc.gov/mmwr/preview/mmwrhtml/ss5601a2.htm

Cook, D. G., & Dunn, W. (1998). Sensory integration for students with autism. In R. L. Simpson & B. S. Myles (Eds.), *Educating children and youth with autism: Strategies for effective practice* (pp. 191–239). Austin, TX: Pro-Ed.

Foley Nicpon, M., Assouline, S. G., & O'Brien, M. (2007, November). *Gifted/talented students on the autism spectrum: Empirically based recommendations for intervention.* Paper presented at the annual convention of the National Association for Gifted Children, Minneapolis, MN.

Gray, C. (1994). *Comic strip conversations.* Arlington, TX: Future Horizons.

Gray, C. (1998). Social stories™ and comic strip conversations with students with Asperger syndrome and high functioning autism. In E. Schopler, G. Mesibov, & L. J. Kunce (Ed.), *Asperger's syndrome or high-functioning autism* (pp. 167–198). New York: Plenum.

Gray, C., & Garand, J. (1993). Social stories: Improving responses of students with autism with accurate social information. *Focus on Autistic Behavior, 8,* 1–10.

Gross, M. (1993). *Exceptionally gifted children.* New York: Routledge.

Gross, M. (2002). Musings: Gifted children and the gift of friendship. *Understanding Our Gifted, 14*(3), 27–29.

Gross, M. (2004, May). *Exceptionally gifted children grown up: Findings from the second decade of a longitudinal study.* Paper presented at the Seventh Biennial meeting of the Wallace Symposium on Talent Development, Iowa City, IA.

Janos, P. M., & Robinson, N. (1985). Psychosocial development in intellectually gifted children. In F. D. Horowitz

& M. O'Brien (Eds.), *The gifted and talented: Developmental perspectives* (pp. 149–195). Washington, DC: American Psychological Association.

Klin, A., Volkmar, F. R., & Sparrow, S. S. (Eds.). (2000). *Asperger syndrome*. New York: Guilford Press.

Luthar, S. S. (1991). Vulnerability and resilience: A study of high-risk adolescents. *Child Development, 62,* 600–616.

Mangrum, C. T., Strichart, S. S., & Latimer, J. (1997). *Peterson's colleges with programs for students with learning disabilities or ADD* (7th ed.). Princeton, NJ: Peterson's Guides.

Mesibov, G. (1984). Social skills training with verbal autistic adolescents and adults: A program model. *Journal of Autism and Developmental Disorders, 14,* 395–404.

Mesibov, G. B., Shea, V., & Schopler, E. (2004). *The TEACCH approach to autism spectrum disorders*. New York: Springer.

National Institute of Mental Health (NIMH). (2008). *Autism spectrum disorders: Pervasive developmental disorders*. Retrieved August 10, 2008, from http://www.nimh.nih.gov/health/publications/autism/complete-publication.shtml

Neihart, M. (2000). Gifted children with Asperger syndrome. *Gifted Child Quarterly, 44,* 222–230.

Neihart, M. (2001). Teaching gifted students with Asperger's syndrome. In F. Rainey & S. Baum (Eds.), *Perspectives in gifted education: Twice exceptional children* (pp. 114–134). Denver, CO: University of Denver.

Neihart, M. (2007). The socioaffective impact of acceleration and ability grouping: Recommendations for best practice. *Gifted Child Quarterly, 51,* 330–341.

Neihart, M., Reis, S. M., Robinson, N. M., & Moon, S. M. (2002). *The social and emotional development of gifted children: What do we know?* Waco, TX: Prufrock Press.

Reis, S., McGuire, J. M., & Neu, T. W. (2000). Compensation strategies used by high-ability students with learning disabilities who succeed in college. *Gifted Child Quarterly, 44,* 123–134.

Reis, S., & Neu, T. (1994). Factors involved in the academic success of high ability university students with learning disabilities. *Journal of Secondary Gifted Education, 5,* 60–74.

Reis, S., Neu, T., & McGuire, J. M. (1997). Case studies of high-ability students with learning disabilities who have achieved. *Exceptional Children, 63,* 463–479.

Rietschel, L. (2000). How did we get here? In A. Klin, F. R. Volkmar, & S. S. Sparrow (Eds.), *Asperger syndrome* (pp. 448–453). New York: Guilford Press.

Rogers, S., Hepburn, S., & Wehner, E. (2003). Parent reports of sensory symptoms in toddlers with autism and those with other developmental disorders. *Journal of Autism and Developmental Disorders, 33,* 631–642.

Sansosti, F. J., & Powell-Smith, K. A. (2006). Using social stories to improve the social behavior of children with Asperger syndrome. *Journal of Positive Behavior Interventions, 8,* 43–57.

Sansosti, F. J., Powell-Smith, K. A., & Kincaid, D. (2004). A research synthesis of social story interventions for children with autism spectrum disorders. *Focus on Autism and Other Developmental Disabilities, 19,* 194–204.

Schissel, P. (1999, Summer). College planning: What you need to know. *The Source, 1,* 4–5.

Sclafani, A. J., & Lynch, M. J. (1995). *College guide for students with learning disabilities.* Miller Place, NY: Laurel Publications.

Silverman, L. K. (Ed.). (1993). *Counseling the gifted and talented.* Denver, CO: Love.

Stewart, K. (2002). *Helping a child with nonverbal learning disorder or Asperger's syndrome.* Oakland, CA: New Harbinger Publications.

Werner, E., & Smith, R. (1992). *Overcoming the odds: High risk children from birth to adulthood.* Ithaca, NY: Cornell University Press.

About the Authors

Maureen Neihart is a licensed clinical child psychologist with more than 25 years of experience working with high-ability children, their families, and their schools. She is the author of *Peak Performance for Smart Kids* and coeditor of the text, *The Social and Emotional Development of Gifted Children: What Do We Know?* Dr. Neihart is a former member of the board of directors of the National Association for Gifted Children and serves on the editorial boards of *Gifted Child Quarterly, Roeper Review,* and *Journal for the Education of the Gifted.* She is associate professor and head of psychological studies at the National Institute of Education, Singapore. Dr. Neihart's special interests include the psychology of talent development, children at risk, and resilience. In her spare time, she fantasizes about living a literary life. Her one act comedy, *The Court Martial of George Armstrong Custer*, was produced and filmed for local television in 2000.

Kenneth Poon is assistant professor of early childhood and special education at the National Institute of Education, Singapore. He received his training in clinical psychology at the University of Queensland, Australia, and obtained a Ph.D. in education from the University of North Carolina at Chapel Hill focusing on autism. He is a trainer in structured teaching, an approach for supporting people with ASD, and trains internationally, supporting parents and professionals in using this approach. He teaches and guest lectures in courses preparing professionals such as teachers, school counselors, speech and language pathologists, and psychologists to support individuals with ASD. Furthermore, he provides consultation services to early intervention programs and specialized settings supporting people with ASD. In addition, he conducts research and publishes widely in peer-reviewed journals as well as books within the field of ASD. His topics of interest include the developmental trajectory, neuropsychological characteristics, behavioral and emotional presentation, and parental aspirations of people with ASD.

Printed in the United States
by Baker & Taylor Publisher Services

Printed in the United States
by Baker & Taylor Publisher Services